T0063026

Being Light Driven

Finding Inner Guidance

Lisa Miliaresis

BALBOA.
PRESS

A DIVISION OF HAY HOUSE

Author Credits: Psychic Medium

Balboa Press books may be ordered through booksellers or by contacting:

Balboa Press
A Division of Hay House
1663 Liberty Drive
Bloomington, IN 47403
www.balboapress.com
1 (877) 407-4847

Because of the dynamic nature of the Internet, any web addresses or links contained in this book may have changed since publication and may no longer be valid. The views expressed in this work are solely those of the author and do not necessarily reflect the views of the publisher, and the publisher hereby disclaims any responsibility for them.

The author of this book does not dispense medical advice or prescribe the use of any technique as a form of treatment for physical, emotional, or medical problems without the advice of a physician, either directly or indirectly. The intent of the author is only to offer information of a general nature to help you in your quest for emotional and spiritual well-being. In the event you use any of the information in this book for yourself, which is your constitutional right, the author and the publisher assume no responsibility for your actions.

Any people depicted in stock imagery provided by Thinkstock are models, and such images are being used for illustrative purposes only. Certain stock imagery © Thinkstock.

Printed in the United States of America.

ISBN: 978-1-4525-1658-5 (sc)
ISBN: 978-1-4525-1659-2 (e)

Balboa Press rev. date: 6/26/2014

Acknowledgement

I thank my family and friends who shared in these light-driven experiences and encouraged me to be true to myself.

My heartfelt appreciation goes out to my spirit guides and all of those from the other side who have put forth their energy to make this healing communication possible.

Contents

Introduction

I am a working wife, mother and grandmother living in a New Jersey suburb. Like most Americans my life is busy and hectic. The difference is that I have had the knowledge that there is life after death. I have spent most of my life hiding my experiences from all except a few friends and family. I was afraid of what others thought of me. I am a medium and have experienced and shared many events that prove there is *life after death*.

Why hide the excitement of communication? Why not scream at the top of my lungs THERE IS LIFE AFTER DEATH? I know, I have seen them, heard them, and communicated. This is exciting news. Just think of what it must be like to have the understanding in your heart, the knowing that when a loved one passes they are not gone! Granted they are not in this physical dimension, but on the emotional highway of love and light in the sky. You can reach them through your thoughts and feelings and most of all your love. Nobody likes to talk about death and/or being without someone they love; it is uncomfortable. The fact of the matter is we all will die. It is just a timing issue. So keep in mind, when death comes, your death day in this dimension is like your birthday into the next. Our lives are eternal and we will transition and be together again.

It is a great feeling to know that we will eventually see each other again but, you may say, what about now?

I miss them, I want to hold their hands and hug them and I can't do that anymore. There are other ways to connect; they are just not in the physical sense. However, the connection is just as powerful. I believe everyone has a degree of ability, some have more than others. The first step is to open your mind to the possibility. After-death communication occurs all the time but many people disregard the subtle communications as coincidence or imagination.

By sharing my experiences I intend to accomplish three things:

1. Bring awareness to all that we don't die, our lives are eternal.
2. Encourage all to meditate and go within to find their own light-driven guidance.
3. Assist others, like myself, who have the ability to communicate, to understand and respect this wonderful responsibility.

Throughout the book you will see italicized paragraphs. This insightful writing comes from the communication of the angel/guide.

May 20, 2005

Express yourself with the intuition of the light. Family, friends and light beings all around you helping you explode your thoughts onto paper. This will happen on its own, watch and see. The experience is golden as are you. Harmony follows and you are chosen to deliver these messages of the light. You are here for us and we are here for you. Excellent! Achieve the highest height. My thoughts and yours will run simultaneously throughout the book and we will create excellent words of hope and harmony. Today is the first day of our union and we will create many things together. My name is of no importance; I am the vibration of light that is your angel/ guide. Acknowledge and accept that which is given. Understand the proofs that are shown and appreciate the love that surrounds us in all forms. This is our way, this is our purpose and through your communications we create much understanding on the higher levels. Communication assists the hereafter as much as it assists those of you on the earth plane. Express and create is our way. Lisa, you will enjoy this project and we will be great. Let's begin.

Part 1

Awakening

Chapter 1

Listen to Your Children

PLEASE LISTEN TO YOUR CHILDREN: Children are sweet and innocent; they have not yet been influenced by society's opinions. Therefore, children are more likely to acknowledge experiences than adults.

I am going to explain what I experienced as a child. Now as an adult looking back on my life I realize what signs were apparent. These signs could easily be mistaken or dismissed but it is important to be aware and listen to your children; don't discourage them or make them fearful. I grew up in the 1960s and during that time, most parents would have no reason to think that their children would be experiencing signs of communication from the other side. The best advice I can give you is to say regular prayers with your children; this will help to comfort you both and protect from any negativity.

I was about four years old, living in a quiet neighborhood of Hillsborough, New Jersey. Many adults have difficulty remembering back to when they were four years old, but I have a very clear recollection of the "WHITE THING". I was always afraid to sleep in darkness and would drive my family crazy because I needed to sleep with my bedroom door open and hallway light on. The fetish became worse after I received frequent visitations from the WHITE THING.

My parents thought I was a typical child with night terrors due to an overactive imagination. They made numerous attempts to calm me down and explain to me that it was only a dream. I would insist that I was not asleep and my eyes were open. My parents would continue to try and calm me down by explaining that it was my imagination playing tricks on me.

This object was a being. It was an illuminating object of light, about eight inches wide and triangular in shape. The light was so bright that it had no tangible end. The light would glow with many rays but I could still see it had a triangular shape. Originally I was ok and calm as long as there was a light on. I did not feel threatened. I was comfortable in my bed and it stayed in the uppermost corner of the room. I never got a feeling of being in danger of any kind. However, after a period of repeated visits, the WHITE THING started to move towards me. I would get startled. Then it not only moved towards me but would hover over me. This made me panic quietly in my bed. I would pull the covers over my head and hide until I could not take it anymore. On occasion, I would feel a vibration. This vibration would occur when the WHITE THING got to close to me. I started to freak out and run into the hallway screaming and insisting the WHITE THING was in my clothes. I must have looked crazy dancing about as if there were a bee on me. I would proceed to stand in the hallway while ranting, raving and taking off my pajamas.

My father finally at his wit's end just desiring a good night's sleep, pretended to stomp on it and flush the WHITE THING down the toilet. The strangest thing happened; the WHITE THING stopped coming to visit me. It was not until later in my life did I realize that the WHITE THING was spirit checking on me.

There were other signs although not as dramatic as the WHITE THING. I remember being about eight years old and seeing images walking around my bedroom, but if I kept the light on I would see them less. This made me more fanatical about sleeping with a light on. There would be times that I would see images on walls and carpets. These images looked like silhouette outlines but they would move. I would keep blinking my eyes to see if I was really seeing this or was it just cracks and bumps on the wall.

Seeing

I thought all children had great imaginations. I was used to hearing my mom trying to explain what was happening to me. She would use the typical explanations such as: probably just the light casting a shadow from the dresser; it was windy out and a tree branch was blowing in the wind; or a passing car would cast a moving shadow from its headlights. Always find some kind of logical excuse for what I was experiencing. This is not her fault; how could she have known what was going on with me, if she never experienced it herself or heard of others who had? During most of my youth I thought everyone saw shadows in their bedrooms at night and had vivid imaginations. I thought that was what allowed children to develop their creative imaginations. I got used to seeing them and as long as they kept some distance I was ok. I wanted the shadow images to stay on the closet door and not come any closer. Most of the time if I mentally asked the images to keep their distance, they did.

When you close your eyes what do you see? Pay attention, it is not only darkness but a mental chalk board. If I relaxed and closed my eyes I saw what appeared to be white smoke that formed symbolic shapes. At an early age I again never thought about it or thought it to be odd that is just the way it was, imagination.

Hearing

I also would occasionally hear voices. This usually would occur when I was almost asleep, just waking or in the bathroom. Thinking back now, it makes sense because at those times you are very relaxed and in a twilight state. (I now know that is the state of mind you must be in order to meditate. To meditate you have to develop the ability to forget about your everyday agenda and relax.) The voices I would hear would come and go very quickly. I would only hear a word or two, not a conversation. For example, if I was in the shower I would hear someone call my name or I would hear hello. I would get out of the bathroom and ask my family who was calling me and ask what they wanted. Of course, no one owned the conversation.

<u>Picture</u>

For some reason if I was to look at a photo for a period of time the image would change. Shadows could cast on it to change hairline, mouth expression and the lips and eyes might move. No big deal! Again I thought it was my imagination.

As I got a little older, around twelve years of age, I noticed that the images were showing me premonitions of a future or past events that took place without my knowledge. From time to time I would tell my mom what I saw and we noticed that within the next few days it would happen. For example, I came downstairs one morning and mentioned that I saw an image of our family dentist and he was waving to me. The next day there was an article in the paper about his death.

I would have premonitions come to me in my dreams. Usually the dreams would provide little insignificant proofs; just enough to let me know the ability is there. Not a straight message for someone.

For example:

1. I would see an object in my dream and a few days later I would either see the object or receive it as a gift.
2. I would dream of an individual that I have not seen in a long time and shortly thereafter I would either hear from them or see them unexpectedly.

By the time I was in my teens logical explanations were not working; there were far too many so-called coincidences that had occurred. Thank goodness Mom was open to the subject, for during these years, 1970's, there was not a lot of information publicly available or at least none that we were aware of. From time to time, we would frequent a local card and palm reader who was recommended to us by friends. This psychic was very interesting and kept us intrigued. Of course I was always told how psychic I was and there were proofs of short-term predictions. He asked me if I knew my spirit guide. I did not even know what a spirit guide was. He explained that everyone has a spirit guide, which is like a guidance counselor, a soul that is there to assist you along your journey. He predicted that I would see my guide soon.

Shortly thereafter I did notice an image of a man on my wall next to my bed. He was flat on the wall and did not have dimension; he wore a turban and I received a thought that he was from India.

I would see him frequently and mentally asked his name. I started to see letters appear on the wall. The letters spelled out the name Theodore. Ok, I now have a spirit guide named Theodore. That was cool! I really did not know what to do but he had a safe comfortable feeling. I liked seeing him and at the beginning I asked questions about my social life, boys and the day-to-day activities of a teen.

Reverend

Through another friend, we heard of a reverend that held frequent sessions in his home. This suburban home would have the people packed outside and down to the street waiting to have their turn with the reverend. His lovely wife would keep people comfortable and warm as they waited on the porch. The porch had hot coffee and cocoa. She would very warmly talk to the people and try to answer their questions about her husband's work. The only compensation was a basket asking for a two-dollar donation.

Inside the home was a modest room with about twenty folding chairs; in the front was a podium and an organ. The reverend was an older gentleman, very tall and slender. Once we arrived early enough to go into the first group. The opening service was very interesting. Universal prayers were said while his wife played the organ. Then the reverend would go into a trance-like state and close his eyes. The rest of the evening was the routine. One at a time he asked the sitters, "May I hear your voice please?"

The sitter would respond, "Good evening, Reverend." Within seconds he started speaking to the sitter about his/her life and perhaps now and then mention spirit and souls that have passed. I was fascinated by this experience. I watched the people one by one be read by the reverend and observed their reactions to what he was saying. Their facial expressions showed that he was touching their hearts with his messages. When each sitter was finished they would leave and another from outside would come in and take his/her chair.

We went back several times each time taking friends. He was always very accurate with us and spoke of events happening in our lives. I don't remember anything that was long term and with me. I was very young so it was usually about school and my emotional turmoil of adolescence.

Meanwhile my own communication skills were developing. I still did not know what I had or how to use it. I only knew it was special. My experiences would become sporadic, meaning there would be a period of time that several premonitions through dreams and visions would occur with frequency then a few months of silence. It was almost as if I was shown a technique and then given a grace period to accept and understand what happened. After a few months passed I thought perhaps I outgrew it; sure enough it would return with a different experience or the same with a greater strength. One of the new experiences was to actually feel the sensation. For example, I had a very difficult day in school and all I wanted to do was go to my room and listen to the radio. As I was walking up the steps towards my room thinking of my aggravating day, I entertained smart-ass remarks I should have said but didn't. All of the sudden I felt a kick in the pants. It was not enough to make me lose my balance but enough to feel as if there were a sudden pressure of a foot against my butt. Well, you could imagine my surprise. This was a first for me to actually feel the sensation of touch so vividly. I thought this was weird because I was still under the impression that all of this was some sort of ESP. It was a little unsettling but all I could do is laugh at the thought of getting reprimanded for my own thoughts.

Teacher

I find myself again in a light-driven situation where we have heard of the perfect opportunity through a so-called chance acquaintance. Mom and I were directed to another interesting person, Jeanette. She held sessions in her residence which was located about twenty minutes from our home. Jeanette was a petite woman, very talented herself but decided not only to do her own work through readings but to teach individuals how to use their abilities correctly. This was perfect and exactly what I needed at that point in my life. So we made the appointment. I did not know what to expect but was excited and nervous at the same time.

I was sitting in her living room waiting for the other students to arrive. We started a conversation; she impressed me as a very sincere individual who spoke of her work with a passion. You could tell from her body language and energy that her heart was in the right place. This gave me an element of trust.

I explained how I had experienced many different types of sensations (visions, sound and overall intuition, etc). She made me relax and spoke to me with a total understanding of all that I have experienced. This was huge. I had never met anyone before that was able to relate to what I had been experiencing. Jeanette told me to keep a pen next to my bed at night for I would be given a message.

What you will read below are events that took place during several visitations to Jeanette, one of which was a private reading.

The other students finally arrived and we proceeded to the dining room. Jeanette was at the head of the rectangular table, Mom to her right, I was to her left and the others were seated around the rectangular table. Jeanette spoke to us about the importance of protection.

The method she recommended was through visualization and prayer. Energy is everywhere; we ourselves give off an energy level. Please understand we all have our own field of energy that surrounds us.

Visualize the White Light of Truth & Love all around you. No harm can come to you for we all are children of God.

There was this white energy force protecting our energy from any negativity. I also remember talking to her privately about protection; it really hit home, because of my own personal realization about the meaning of prayer.

I always understood prayer even if it wasn't the conventional method of organized religion. When I went to synagogue much of our prayers were in Hebrew, which I did not understand. I could never get into other people's words written in a prayer book whether they were English or Hebrew. There were a few prayers I really liked but for the most part I would just repeat the words, for that's all they were, just words. They felt meaningless because they were not mine. Then I started to create and say my own prayers, silently. These prayers would make sense to me. They were my words with God. When I spoke to God from what was within my heart it carried meaning and made me feel whole.

Jeanette proceeded to say protection prayers for all of us. Once we were all safely set the class began. She explained that there were many ways to connect. Listed below are several methods she spoke of:

Always protect yourself with protection prayer before you start (See appendix A) and give thanks when you finish.

<u>Automatic Writing</u> -
Automatic writing is an effective way
to connect to your higher self.

1. Protection prayer always before you begin.
2. Hold a pen or pencil in your hand very loosely, almost not touching it all.
3. Sit up straight with your feet flat on the floor. (Do not cross your legs.)
4. Ask a simple specific question in your head. (At first try for a yes or no question.)
5. Watch to see if your hand moves. (Only two or three of us had movement right away.)
6. Give thanks. (Show appreciation.)

Of course, being our first time the pen created only squiggles. Jeanette explained that it would start like squiggles on a paper then turn to drawings or words and ultimately if it was correct for you it could become a tool for further understanding.

<u>Psychometry</u>

We paired up to practice psychometry. Each of us had a partner we did not know. Psychometry is when you hold an object and read the energy from that object.

1. Protection prayer always before you begin.
2. Hold a small object in your hand (jewelry, photo, note, etc.) This object should belong to

someone else and perhaps someone you don't know.
3. Close your eyes and focus on that object.
4. Explain what you feel, see, smell etc.

I don't remember the details but I do remember being surprised by the accuracy of information received. There was no way the students could have known this information; we did not even know each other.

This was really cool, just the thought that this is all possible.

A Little Weird

We returned to our original chairs and she turned off the lights. Because of our previous conversation, Jeanette knew I was uncomfortable in darkness, but she convinced me to calm myself. Plus I could see the street light was seeping through the dining room window. Jeanette told us to look around the room and one by one she wanted us to stand up and explain what we saw or experienced.

Most of the students saw colored orbs or flashes of light. I saw the lights but also saw images and was instructed to tell about the most vivid. I explained that there was a man in a checkered jacket, with a mustache and there were kitchen curtains next to him. I received the thought that there was something new about the curtains and he liked them. Jeanette got very excited because I described her late husband and she just completed changing her kitchen curtains.

There was another student that started to speak in a voice that was not her own. I found this a little creepy. She told another student very pertinent information but as she did so her voice and demeanor would change. Then she looked at my mom and laughed. She explained in her own voice, "You just recently received a very unusual gift from a man, a toilet seat!" This was true; my dad was visiting and he noticed one of our toilet seats was broken so he left for a while and returned with a new one.

It was Jeanette's turn. She looked at Mom and said, "I know your boyfriend. I have his photo in my bedroom." Not exactly the words a woman wants to hear from a psychic. Jeanette left the room to get the photo and we all just look at each other. Sure enough she brings back a photo that was taken at a dinner dance and there is Mom's friend at the next table. She was very impressive.

This was a great experience for me but our financial situation and schedule did not permit us to continue our sessions with Jeanette. I was grateful to Jeanette and my mom, Jeanette for sharing her knowledge with others and Mom for supporting me with this interest.

Mom loved the idea that her daughter could do special things. She would occasionally bring friends or coworkers home to try psychometry. I liked the idea of having experience with people I was not familiar with. I would hold their ring or object and read the vibrations from it. Each time there was substantial validity to what I received. I remember one occasion where I told this one woman she was due for some good fortune in her life and as a proof gave her three numbers. She played the numbers in the lottery the next day and sure enough won a few hundred dollars.

This gift/responsibility is not for picking numbers from the lottery; this was given as a proof. I have been given numbers several times in my life but each time it was for a proof of a greater message and never enough finance to change my life.

As my automatic writing progressed Theodore was not as visible. I knew I was still protected and guided but I did not see him as often. Automatic writing became second nature to me. My pen would move freely about the paper with scribbles that had words in them. Most of all they gave me thoughts that I had to learn to trust. I did this for many years and was always amazed at the accuracy. There were times when I would draw an object. I recall drawing a ring that looked like a flower and saw a blue sparkle in the middle. Sure enough two months down the road the same ring was given to me as a gift. This became a tool that was comfortable for me. There were times when the writing was not in my hand but that of a lefty, written upside down or of an unusual slant.

Clairaudience is an awareness that is projected to you through hearing.

Well at the time Jeannette mentioned to me that I would be awakened in the middle of the night to receive a message, I did not think much of it. It was not unusual for me to be awakened but I usually saw images talking to me or on occasion shadows/souls. Needless to say, I did not take her words lightly and I did place a pen and paper next to my bed.

<u>A New Audio Experience</u>

About two weeks later I started to experience a strange sensation in my ears. First the right ear I would hear a tone that would ring and apply slight pressure then stop. This was not all the time but frequent enough to be noticeable. Then the same thing would frequent the left ear. Well again I just dismissed this sensation thinking perhaps I had water in my ears from the shower.

One night I experienced the sensation again in my right ear. This time it was stronger. A few minutes later I saw a flash. It looked like a lightning bolt, but it was an extremely bright light. In an instant this bolt went straight to my ear. I was calm and thinking back I wonder why? I felt the love in my heart and did not get the feeling of fear. A few days latter it happened. I was asleep and was awakened by the tone in my ear again but this time I hear a voice that said, "258 you won $800." I received the understanding that I was going to win this money. Then I saw a projection of myself as a bride and the guy looked familiar. It was a guy I just started to date! Marriage was the furthest thing from my mind. We worked together in a local diner and really liked one another, but marriage? I will put that thought out of my mind. A week passed and I went on with my day-to-day activities (school and work). I was in my class and not very interested in my work. I was trying not to fall asleep, but my eyes were closing. When my eyes were closed I saw with the white smoke as clear as day it spelled out "Tonight is the night". My eyes popped open and I could not believe this. I closed my eyes again and saw the three numbers from my clairaudience experience. So I wrote the three numbers on my hand so I would not forget. That night I had a date but was not sure where we were going. I ended up at the racetrack. I knew the numbers were given to me to play. Obviously, I could not tell my date about the visions I experienced. For fear it would have been our last date. So I told him I had a dream and in my dream I saw the three numbers which were now written on my hand. He laughed and thought I was cute. I told him in my dream I won $800.

Lo and behold in the evening races there were two trifectas, one early in the evening and one at the end of the evening. (A trifecta is a race where you pick the first three horses.) I used the three numbers from my dream and boxed them. By boxing the numbers I had an opportunity to win no matter which order the horses came in as long as they were the first three. The first trifecta came and went and I did not win. I waited for the last trifecta race and boxed them again. This time my date was really laughing because the numbers I wrote were long shots and he didn't think I had a chance. I said I had to try anyway because it was given to me. Lo and behold my three numbers won. I won a little over $1,000 but after taxes I walked away with $800. The $800 was just what I needed to pay my tuition at county college. We were both amazed. A year and a half later we were engaged and eventually married.

Chapter 2

More than ESP

<u>Martial Arts?</u>

I was married with one child, a two-year-old son. I recall being very emotional because I went from being a very active young woman to a stay-at¬home mom with no car. Don't get me wrong, I loved being a mom and realized it is the most important and rewarding activity in the world. I was just young and going through a life event change, being stir crazy. I had always been on the slender side and now I had a weight problem as well as adjusting to my new lifestyle. My morale was a little low. I recall very clearly seeing a vision. This vision was very distinct. Everyone's face and body were clear as day. I received a thought that at the time this vision becomes a reality I would be healed of my current emotional predicament.

<u>Vision</u>

I saw myself in a karate uniform along with my son, the karate master, and a young girl about eight. There was also a baby girl in the karate master's arms but there was an X fading on and off of her. I was visibly older and thinner, my son was several years older and the girl next to him I felt as my daughter (but at the time only had the one child). I could not even imagine taking karate and the thought of it made me laugh. That little one in the karate master's arm puzzled me. But why was there an X on her fading in and out? It gave me a peculiar feeling; seeing that, I had the impression that she was either my child or I loved her like my own child.

I reacted to this vision as I usually did and put this vision in the back of my mind and went on with my day-to-day activities of life.

About a year later I gave birth to a beautiful little girl. Two years later while my son was in preschool he participated in a martial arts orientation program. Once the program was finished I enrolled my son in the local martial arts, Tang So Do school. At that time I was involved with an aerobics program and very bored so I jumped at the opportunity to participate in the karate. Tang So Do is for all ages. This was great! I could participate in an activity with my son, as well as get in shape and learn self-defense. Martial arts was a win/win situation. This became a passion of mine and a way of life. We continued our training at the school for thirteen years. My daughter eventually started her karate training when she reached the age of six. I will explain later the significance of the baby with the X.

Looking back on to my training I realize how much martial arts assisted me in my mediumship abilities today. To mention a few attributes: respect, focus and confidence.

Respect—is a must. You must first give respect to others if you expect them to respect you in return (law of attraction).

- ◆ Some people call mediumship a gift but in reality it is a responsibility. Through meditation I have received many lessons and messages that are of a much higher vibration than ours. Always a product of pure love and sincerity, this energy deserves the highest vibration of respect.

Focus—the ability to focus and concentrate while many distractions are going on around you.

- ◆ When channeling you must be able to focus on the communication even when there are distractions, similar to carrying on more than one conversation at a time.

Confidence—belief in yourself.

- ◆ To be a medium you must have confidence in order to trust the information which is given to you. The communication is very subtle and you must be able to determine the difference between communication and your own thought.
- ◆ It takes a great deal of confidence to trust the information that is given. These messages are from the light (high power of goodness/Godlike). To doubt the communication would be like doubting the source from which they came.

To give you an example of where focus and confidence take place in martial arts, a student is asked to break a wood board. The purpose is not to show how strong you are but a mental game of mind over matter. The student must actually visualize and think through the wood. You must open your mind beyond that which is visible and concentrate on punching a target point on the other side of the wood. What you see does not matter if you believe in yourself.

A Medium Is Not Supposed to Know Everything About Their Own Lives

What about the baby in the karate master's arms? Messages are so deep when they are received and can take a period of time to unfold. The spirit world has no understanding of time. Their dimension is of a vibration of light and much faster than ours. Therefore, it is difficult to determine past, present and future. What may seem to be a lifetime to us may only be a matter of hours to those in spirit.

The original vision was in 1984. I gave birth to my daughter in 1985. We started martial arts in 1986 and did get back into better physical shape. During this time I had been using automatic writing as my tool of choice and began making connections to my higher self. To make a long story short, during this time, my oldest brother had gone through a very difficult divorce. He had three beautiful children from this marriage and was getting his life back together. My prayers and thoughts were always with him and the children for love and happiness. He found happiness with a lovely woman who had three children of her own from a previous marriage. (They later married.) My automatic writing became very forceful and continued with the same message. Surprise! Surprise is coming! My brother was on my mind. I would ask what surprise! Then I received Baby! Well I thought this surprise baby was for my brother who had three children of his own and his future wife had three of her own. My initial thought was that was all he needs is to have another child! So, I warned him! This continued on for about six months. I think I drove my brother and future sister-in-law crazy while scaring them half to death. At this time my son was eleven and my daughter was seven and I decided to move on with my own career and life. I entertained the thought of getting my tubes tied. I consulted my doctor and decided once I returned from vacation I would get the procedure done. Well, I returned home to find out I was with child. Needless to say this baby girl was a big surprise. She is our blessing and I could not imagine my family's life without her.

My interpretation of the baby and the fading X is that her existence in this world was not yet determined and that is why the X was fading in and out. I am so glad she decided to join us.

New Spirit Guide

Time had passed since I had been practicing automatic writing. Theodore's visits diminished and I sensed a new spirit guide. This spirit guide did not provide me with a name but a vibration. I could tell this was my guide by the comfort level I felt. At this point in time communication was not an everyday occurrence. I would still be given intervals of information and experiences that would go strong for a few weeks then back off a few weeks or months. I remember being confused by the inconsistency but looking back now I realize it was through these experiences I was being gradually educated.

In 1994 we had just moved into our new home and this was a very exciting time for us. I had a hectic and demanding schedule as a working mother of three. At the end of the day when I got into bed, my head was not on the pillow more than five minutes and I was out like a light.

There were several very interesting events that happened to me over a period of a few years. Not everyone in my family was accepting of these wonderful experiences so if I had to share a vision or experience with someone that was close-minded I would refer to the experience as a dream. I knew it was not a dream but for those that fear what they don't understand it was a good way to explain a communication without freaking anyone out. I did not like hiding things because I have always been a very straightforward person who speaks her mind. I prayed for directions on this topic and was always given the same message, BE PATIENT. At this time in my life there were only a few people that I felt comfortable enough to confide in (Florence, who is a close friend, my mother, sister and sisters-in-law).

Some of my experiences are noted below:

- I awoke just as the morning light was seeping into the windows, to see a life-size knight in shining armor standing next to my bed watching me sleep. As I focused my eyes to get a clearer view he tipped his visor at me and disappeared. This knight communicated to me through both thought and feeling. I knew that he was there protecting me while I slept. I was elated at the thought I was being looked after. This image was different than the ones I have seen in the past. It was no longer on the wall in two-dimensional forms, but was free standing and three-dimensional. It was clear, but translucent, looking like an ice sculpture.

- It is common to have the same dream over and over again. I however had a repetitive vision; I would find myself waking up to see a floating window pane with many people/souls on the other side of the window trying to talk to me. They looked like normal people only they were translucent. Their mouths were moving but I could not hear anything. Nonetheless this would leave me perplexed. I did not understand why this was happening and what I was supposed to do about it. I would pray for clarity. I now understand that the souls were showing me that they wanted to communicate. Communication is just as healing for those in the afterlife as it is for us on the Earth plane.

- Every night before bed I recited a prayer of protection: "The white light of truth surrounds us; no harm will come to us for we are all children of God." Then I would continue with my prayers.

On December 7, 1999, there was an unusual occurrence. This night I was lying on my back in bed with my eyes closed just waiting for sleep. I went to stretch my head backwards on the pillow and as I stretched I saw a huge white beam of light. This beam was so big that my head seemed to touch only the outskirts of it and I experienced a vibrating sensation. My first reaction was to tilt my head forward and as I did the light dimmed. I immediately tilted it back again and experienced the same vibration and the brightness returned to the huge light. This all happened so very fast and I was reacting without thought, only on my natural reflexes. As I started to realize what was going on, I thought it must have been the night table lamp left on. Then suddenly the beam disappeared. I opened my eyes to notice the light had already been off.

That next day I could not think of anything else but this experience. To have an unexplained occurrence leaves you on an exuberant high. I decided to research this experience on the internet. I did not find anything concrete so I went to a respected professional, George Anderson. Through George Anderson's web site I realized my questions could be addressed. Either he or a member of his staff would answer me via email. I emailed my experience asked if this ever happened to him and if it did what was his interpretation of the experience. I received an answer:

> "This type of thing happens all the time. It is only your loved ones who still take an interest in your life and are around like guardians. Perhaps they

just came by to check on you. It's nice to know that our loved ones still care for us on the Earth and look out for our well-being. Remember to say thanks to them!"

♦   I heard a buzzing noise in my ear and awoke to see this beautiful angelic image. I think it was female with very short hair and delicate features. She floated closer, was visible from her waist up and surrounded by a white mist. My heart was beating a mile a minute but I dared not speak. I was so excited I did not want her to leave without explaining why she was there. She spoke to me telepathically and said, "Don't be afraid." I could not help it; my heart was still racing but her vibration was so soft and calming I settled the best I could. She said, "You're going to be used like a telephone." I could not keep my mind calm to listen, instead I silently asked about my life and my husband's health. She said, "You are not to know everything about yourself or you would ruin your sweet life." Then she proceeded to give me a protocol.

  1. Always tell the truth.
  2. Don't be judgmental of others.
  3. Be respectful.

Every time I receive a message it is just as exciting as the first time. I never take communication for granted. What can be difficult to understand is how to interpret the communication. The symbolic communication provided by Spirit is accurate; however the human discernment can be misunderstood. There is no sense of time in the spirit world, therefore learning how to be patient is a necessity. There is no sense of past, present or future; time blends.

I had a desire to learn but continuing my education was not simple. There were times I felt very alone on my journey as if I lived in a cave. I longed to understand myself and what purpose I could possible have. I knew this ability/responsibility was special but I did not know where to find a school that would teach me how to use my abilities and enhance them to their highest potential. Nor would my lifestyle permit me to take that kind of time for myself. Perhaps that was part of my journey, to be guided by spirit. What I did realize was that I had access to books. Over the years I found I was light driven by spirit to that direction.

Chapter 3

Coming Out

Siblings

Siblings in my family are very tight. We all do not live near one another nor do we speak daily and currently one of my sibling lives in the hereafter. Nonetheless the life line of love is strong. There are four in my family and we are all different, each one with an ingredient that adds to this recipe of loving unity. The adult relationships as they are, we know if one of us is in need we will rally and do all that is in our power to assist. There is never a doubt of honesty or trust. If one asks a question we reply with our honest sincere opinion whether it is wanted or not.

I am going to continue to speak of my younger sister Amy. When we were young and living under the same roof we were like oil and vinegar. She was very loving, however difficult. I find that the relationships we have with our siblings contributed to the adults we have become. Amy does not share in my ability to communicate with the other side; however, she has a much better ability than I at verbalizing her opinion to those in this dimension. Her communication skills are one of her many strengths. She thinks on her feet and is capable of handling the most impossible situations with a quick clarity.

When I would talk of reading others, Amy would caution me about protecting my family and encourage me to change my last name. Even though she was supportive, her protective instincts kicked into overdrive. Amy was very right-brained and needed a reason for everything. All of her life she witnessed my abilities and found there to be too many situations and validations to call coincidence. At the time of my coming out and decision to go public my sister was extremely supportive of me. However, she was very cautious of others' opinions and did not want me or my children to fall victim to ridicule.

Spirit loves to multitask, if it were not for the following chain of events my sister would not have realized first hand the value of the work.

One night Amy called and wanted a reading. I balked a little about the timing of her call, but I gave in. Amy was in the middle of transitions with job and matters of the heart and clearly expected to hear a little about herself. What happened next took both of us by surprise.

A female presence made herself known and clearly stated that this information was intended for Amy's best friend Fran. The female presence was extremely strong. Her name was Mary (Fran's Aunt). Amy and I both felt as if ice water were running down our backs. I had not known about Fran's Aunt Mary but Amy did. She had been brutally murdered a few years back. Mary came through with other family members. I immediately told Amy to write everything down so she could relay the entire message to Fran. Amy was very close with Fran and her big Italian family. They are devout Catholics and Amy was extremely reluctant about mentioning my abilities, let alone delivering messages. She kept saying, "I am not going to lose my best friend over this." Mary's presence was very strong and loving. She came through with the other relatives giving validations of a specific nature. From names, describing objects of hers that were given to family members (scarf, blanket, jewelry). Plus the most important message of all, she would be assisting Fran's mother to cross into the hereafter. Fran's mother at that time was suffering with cancer.

Amy was now caught in a dilemma. She was given the obligation of passing on this information to her dear friend who was currently going through the toughest of times. Amy knew her friend was stressed and upset with the weight of the world on her shoulders and did not want to do or say anything to upset her further. At the end of the call I told Amy this is so much bigger than the two of us or even Fran. I would leave this information with her and advise her to find the opportunity to pass it on to Fran. In my lifetime I have had the obligation of passing on information to those who had no concept of such communication. I would say I had a dream and deliver my message. Amy found the strength to talk to Fran. To Amy's surprise Fran was very accepting and grateful for this communication. Fran was able to confirm many validations and of course found great comfort in the main message that Mary was well in the hereafter and would be assisting Fran's mother soon into the world of spirit.

This information now became Fran's responsibility to decide whether or not to share with her large family including her mother. The decision was easy for Fran; because of the communication Fran felt a tremendous comfort and understanding. She now knew without a doubt that we continue our lives in the hereafter and Aunt Mary will be there for the family just as she was during her existence here in this dimension.

Spirit's hand multitasks with a domino effect. Over the course of at least a year the illness took its toll on Fran's Mom and she eventually passed on. Fran and her sisters were preparing for the funeral. Their mom always took great pride in her appearance and they wanted to be sure that she was presented in the best possible way. They grabbed a few accessories from her room, one of which was a pink scarf from her drawer. As they tied the scarf around her neck they noticed an embroidered initial M on it. How appropriate this scarf had once belonged to Aunt Mary.

The day of the funeral I went with Amy to pay our respects. As Amy and I were leaving, Aunt Mary came to give me a message letting the family know that their mom arrived and was still participating in their love. I described a scene; a beautiful body of water like a lake and a dock where her mom saw all the children sitting on the dock. Amy called Fran the next day and mentioned the communication and validation. This message meant a great deal to Fran because the family gathered after the funeral at her brother's house (I had never been there nor did I know about it). His home backed up against a lake with a dock and that day all the children were sitting on the dock. This experience was the most comforting and meaningful of all to Fran and made the whole experience a little easier.

Amy was given a true first hand experience and understanding of helping those she loved by delivering the messages, the true purpose communication holds.

Fran was amazed along with other family members. She always believed in Heaven but now felt comfort in knowing her mom and aunt are together. Amy, Fran, Fran's sisters and I would gather regularly for dinner and reminisce. Occasionally we are blessed with a visit from Aunt Mary and Fran's mom.

For me, the timing was amazing. I had been struggling with whether or not to tell others about my ability. I was able to clearly see how the work of communication was my purpose. I needed my sister's support and strength to go public and these messages allowed her to experience the connection of spirit first hand, instilling the emotional depth of the messages.

It was communicated to me through meditation that 12% of all people have this ability but only a few recognize and enhance it. Out of those few a smaller percentage uses the ability to assist others.

My coming out happened over a period of a few years and a very large portion of my confidence came when I met Keila. I was working full time at a local insurance brokerage company when Keila, a young beautiful girl, joined our company. Our company was not huge but it was large enough where you could work at the same place for days on end and not run into each other. However, spirit was multitasking again, Keila ended up sitting in my area. Keila was a friendly girl with lots of personality, or should I say spirit. She worked very hard while attending school in the evening. Her recent purchase of a townhouse brought about some significant changes in her life. She purchased this home with the intention of bringing her son and parents over from Puerto Rico. At the time of her move she noticed many energy changes around her. She would come to work very excited, speaking to anyone who would listen about the ghosts in her new home and the phenomena that were occurring. Some of these unexplainable occurrences were: electrical appliances with a mind of their own turning on and off, walking into a room of white mist, dreams occurring waking her in the middle of the night then sensing a presence next to her, and one of our favorites was she looked in the mirror to see the back of her hair standing straight up as if someone was playing with it.

Keila would come to work in a frantic state and could not sleep at the home. She would end up going to her aunt's house in order to get a good night's sleep. She had the house blessed and sprinkled with holy water but to no avail; she still had visitors. I could not help but overhear her. At this time I still told no one at work of my abilities. I did not tell others that I see and speak to the dead; it would not be professional. Instead I shared my knowledge with others by talking of books I read and I organized a trip to New York, where George Anderson, a well-known medium, was holding a workshop.

I confronted Keila about these occurrences and told her she was not alone many people have had experiences like this, and not to be afraid. Her fear was only making things worse and not getting to the understanding of what was going on. There had to be a reason the souls were rallying around her at this time. I then proceeded to tell her how I too see, feel, and communicate to those on the other side. I gave her my first influential book, We Don't Die by George Anderson. Keila was so relieved to hear my stories of communication, however she still was not comfortable in her new home. She asked me to go to her home and to see if I could receive; I agreed. Keila lived close to our work so we went at lunch time. Once in her home I immediately understood the presence of family; the souls were so happy to have their communications heard and understood. Many validations were received from her grandparents and others in family members. Her grandmother loved to play with her hair and that is why it was standing up in the mirror. Grandma was playing with it. By reading Keila, she was now able to experience the communication through love instead of fear. Keila was embarking upon a new crossroad in her life. This crossroad had to deal with balance, understanding of her ability and assisting her family (mom, dad and son). Those in the hereafter had to add their two cents and support. You realize not all people embarking on a new venture have these experiences. Keila of course has mediumship abilities. Her childhood was difficult and filled with many old-fashioned superstitions. This caused her to fear and suppressed her energy. By her suppressing the abilities her energy did not go away but just waited for her to come to a point in her life where she could try again. Instead of a gradually awakening and understanding as I experienced, Keila seemed to have experienced a build-up and then eruption. I had to assist her in controlling and understanding this ability/responsibility without fear. We immediately developed a friendship that felt as if we knew each other forever. It was wonderful for both of us to find another to share in our experiences. Keila was a quick study but this was a process and did not happen overnight. Her thirst for knowledge kept her reading and I suggested she start meditating. This was a challenge for Keila being a working mom and student who burned the candle at both ends. She did not always keep the steady practice of meditation.

While working we attended numerous meetings; these meetings were held in a good size conference room. We enjoyed looking around the room which was full of energy, observing the souls and receiving messages. We would separately write notes and afterwards compare what we experienced in the room. The souls would appear to both of us and deliver messages as if teaching us tools. Both of us seeing the same souls gave me confidence and her courage. They were multitasking again.

Over a period of two years time through the guidance of spirit, Keila has overcome her lifelong fear. I explained the importance of meditating on a regular basis; this would give spirit time to communicate while allowing Keila her time for uninterrupted daily activity. In the beginning Keila was very fearful and stubborn. Spirit showed patience and love as confirmation after confirmation would transpire between the two of us. I would meditate each morning and Keila did not always make the time for meditations. However, she was subjected to much dream activity and developed interpretation from spirit. As we compared our experiences they would complement each other. My deceased brother would come to her with a message for me confirming what I received during my morning meditation. I would receive a message from angels and relatives acknowledging her communications. Spirit was helping us help each other. She was conquering her fears and being taught to trust more in God and herself and I was conquering my fear of exposure and trusting in God and my life purpose. People around us could not help but overhear our conversation and slowly but surely I was coming out. Friends wanted me to come to their homes and read their families.

Now you must understand life is like a three-ring circus. Things are going on simultaneously. Keila and I helping each other, Amy, Fran and Aunt Mary, my visit with angels and confirmation of that visit through Michele Livingston (later in chapter 4) and much more I was not even aware of at that time.

It was communicated to me during meditation that I was coming to a fork in my life and a decision would have to be made. Either I would continue to only help the select few (family and friends) or help many.

A few months back I was light driven to hear about a local seminar with Michele Livingston. I liked to share these experiences and arranged a group. There was a last-minute cancellation of one of our group members and I persuaded my sister to join us.

That day my sister received a meaningful message from my grandparents. Amy had received many messages through me before but to have someone without knowledge of her or her family deliver the message was icing on the cake. During a break I went to see another on the other side of the room. My family was speaking about me and my abilities when a very nice woman who was sitting in the next row turned and asked my mom if she thought I would read her. When I returned to the rest of the group and got settled my mom told me what had happened. Of course, I immediately thought of my previous meditation and accepted. Once the seminar was complete I met the lady in the back of the room where I conducted the reading. She was very appreciative and wanted to contact me so we exchanged email addresses. I received a very nice email shortly thereafter where she expressed her appreciation and acknowledged numerous validations that were given. From there requests were made for me to read others at her home and I agreed thinking of my purpose. Of course my sister, the protector, came with me.

When I first started reading groups I would get nervous and think to myself what if nothing comes through? I should at least bring a cake (that was never an issue). People out of appreciation wanted to pay me and I was not ready for this even though I could use the money. I asked Amy, who knew how to make things happen, if there was a way I did not have to handle money and it could go to the AIDS Fund in our Brother Danny's name. Of course, within minutes Amy had a contact that supplied us with envelopes that could be mailed directly from the people to the AIDS Fund in honor of Danny. I would give the envelopes to the sitters and they would send in any amount of money they saw fit. Amy would get a note from the AIDS Fund that a donation was made. This allowed me to feel good about myself and what I was doing while gaining experience. This was a great temporary fix that was a positive for everyone. However, as the demand increased I had to come up with a way that I could continue to read and not travel, putting my sister out as well as myself and family. I decided to incorporate, and formed Extreme Communication LLC (www.2communicate.net).

This allowed me to rent a room at a local hotel, now charging for my seminars. I have been blessed with the best light-driven advisors—spirit! I would get nervous at the thought of taking this big step and spirit would always let me know when I was on the right track. When I was younger I would be light driven by spirit to books and programs. By this time I would be directed by electronic signs and communication though blocks of thought. Being insecure it took a great deal of courage for me to incorporate and move forward. I would take a step forward and notice the sign of approval. My car's clock radio would go screwy. I would leave work for lunch at 1:00 P.M., go to run an errand which took only fifteen minutes, get back into my car and now the clock read 8:30 P.M. or all of my programmed radio stations would be all mixed up. I could tell when others were talking about their validations. Spirits communicated to me, "You're famous"; it made me chuckle just the thought of that. Sometimes I would just walk and feel my short five foot one inch body as if I were six feet tall. One day I was going to the hotel where I now hold my sessions to set up an account. I was nervous and my heart was pounding a mile a minute. I almost called Keila to ask her opinion but stopped myself because I knew I must trust in myself and this was the right thing to do. No sooner than I completed this transaction did Keila call me with a message from spirit. They told her she must call me today and tell me I was not alone. Spirit would be guiding me every step of the way and to continue because it is my purpose.

The light-driven energy guides me all the way which brings me to the title of this book, for if each and every one of us took the time to sit quietly and meditate, go within, you to could sense and acknowledge your light-driven paths. It is special and feels great. I hope through this book I can share this feeling with all of you.

Part 2

Confirmation

Chapter 4

Prayer

How to express prayer

June 12, 2005

Happiness, harmony and health are all big reasons for prayer. The bottom line is prayer exceeds in lifting your energy to levels of unexpected heights.

Your own ability within can capture the essence of life. Continue to challenge and be challenged, succeed with your triumphs over and over until the end of this life. For here is where we learn and grow faster. Encourage others to challenge themselves to reach their highest possible level of light. For that is our soul's goal. Light enrichment!

Everything is energy, especially our thoughts and prayers. This energy puts forth motion that can manifest physical outcomes. There is no doubt in my mind that our prayers are heard by spirit and affect our lives.

Prayer Is a Direct Dial—June and Barbara

I would like to tell you about the first time I was sure my prayers were being heard and answered. This story needs a little background so please bear with me.

One day I was relaxing in my living room after work, all of the sudden I heard a pressure noise in my ear. When I looked up, I saw a beautiful white full body image of woman. This woman was not flat, but 3D and had a familiar face. Her face was not clear and I could not place her. I felt a very strong emotion of love from this energy. She waved to me, blew me a kiss and floated out. An hour later I received a call from mom that one of her best friends, as well as mine, had passed suddenly of a stroke. Our friend's name was June. I realized then it was her who blew me a kiss goodbye.

June had always been a strong woman; she and my mom had been divorcées at a time when it was not popular. Our families spent many holidays together and she loved me as if I were her own.

There was another woman I had just met and became very friendly with. Her name was Barbara. Barbara and I met as we commuted back and forth from New Jersey to Philadelphia every day on the bus. She was very kind and took me under her wing. Barbara was a breast cancer survivor. Barbara had surgery a few years prior and was full of life. Barbara had a lovely daughter from her first marriage and was remarried. She and her husband just completed the process of adopting another child. One year later the cancer came back fast and furious. Barbara tried everything from chemotherapy to a macrobiotic diet but it was too late.

Time passed and she was in the ending stages in the hospital. I am one of those people that cannot handle when others are sick. I don't know how to respond. Not because I don't feel for the sickly, I just can't handle it. So imagine if you will, I am trying to prepare myself for the next day when I am going to the hospital to visit my dying friend. I was saying my prayers and I knew Barbara was not going to live. I also knew Barbara was afraid to die. As I prayed that night I did not ask God to repair her health and make her well for I knew her illness was terminal and at the very end. Instead I asked God to protect and love her but I also asked June, who I knew to be strong and loving, to go to Barbara and help her into the light where she could rest in peace with God. (Now keep in mind June and Barbara never knew each other in life). I closed my eyes and saw what looked like a deformed image of Barbara. Her nose was narrow, face drawn and her fingers were skeletal. The next day came, and I was in the hospital room with my friend, her daughter and husband. Barbara looked just like my vision from the night before. By seeing her image the night before, I did not react poorly, and instead could concentrate on Barbara, not my anxieties. She was lying back in her bed and sedated with morphine. All of a sudden she sat up in her bed, looked at me and said, "June is here." Barbara then plopped back in her bed. I was amazed! This was proof that my prayers were heard the night before and Barbara would make it into the light just fine. Soon after, I went for coffee with Barbara's daughter and husband and told them of my prayers, etc. I asked if they or Barbara knew of anyone with name June. They both said no. They did not think it was anything special and stated that she has been highly sedated and very afraid. To me however, this was something I will never forget and June and Barbara will always be in my prayers.

<u>Angels Are Among Us</u>

There have been many times when I have had proof of my prayers being heard. This example took place over a period of one year's time. Just to give you a little background, my home is where my entire family has and will always be welcome each Thanksgiving. A few years back my oldest brother went through a very messy divorce and his ex-wife made it very difficult for him to share holidays with his three children. There were times that the courts would agree the kids should be with their father and she would manage to keep them from him one way or another. Our children lived in separate states and always looked forward to seeing one another at this time of year.

This particular Thanksgiving my brother had come without the kids. The entire weekend I saw the sadness in his eyes. I found myself again asking God through prayer to assist my brother and his children with a loving bond of family unity. May this union be of love and of greatest possible good for each of them! I prayed that the boys and my brother be able to appreciate and love each other freely.

I was exhausted from entertaining and slept soundly; however, as I was waking I saw a vision of two beautiful angels conjoined and in a golden picture frame. This vision was different because the angels were very clear, three dimensional with a golden glow around them. The angels moved inside of the frame similar to the pictures in the Harry Potter movie. The angels communicated to me that the union had begun and the kids would return to him. Keep in mind this was November. I told my brother of this vision and felt uplifted.

A few months passed and it was March. I did not see or hear of much improvement so I started to get discouraged with the angels and their message. I prayed again and said, "I don't mind giving messages to others but did not want to give people messages of false hopes." I then received communication from my other brother Dan, who passed a few years ago, and my grandfather who also passed. They came together to deliver communication to me. I was told not to give up hope and to be patient. Then I was directed to call my mother and tell her that both my grandfather and brother are fine and around. I gave her several validations that she could understand right away. Then there was another message I was told that the unity of my brother's family was a strong message and lesson we should not give up our faith. A validation was given to my mother that on the other side of her bed an electronic object would turn on by itself. *Look for this to happen, it would be your proof of the family union.* Mom said, "I only have a TV in my room and that is on the same side of the bed that I sleep on."

Spring time, I had another light-driven moment where I turned on the TV, channel 8 that I don't usually watch, and saw Michele Livingston. Michele is also a medium. I had never heard of her but I liked what I saw; she seemed to be sincere and similar to me. I looked her up on the internet and saw that she would be giving a seminar in my home town this coming June right before Father's Day. I took this to be a light-driven moment and a group of us signed up. My mother would be coming to visit around the same time. She always came to visit this time of year and was able to visit with the family, see my girls in their dance recitals plus go to the seminar.

Beginning of June, I was with a coworker and on a shelf away from all, sits a clock radio. This radio turned on by itself and started to play music. (Electronic occurrences are not new to me; I know it is spirit trying to let me know that they are present and something of importance is about to go down.) We both laughed and said it must be my brother Dan, who has shared his presence with us before.

That morning I spoke to my mother and she exclaimed that she wanted to call me last night but it was too late. There was a clock radio in her bedroom; she totally forgot about it. The clock radio is on the other side of her bed. She forgot about it because she only used if for clock purposes and never touched it. All of a sudden, the night before it started to play music. She had completely forgotten about our phone conversation and the validation given until that moment. That was the validation and she could not wait to tell me.

Mom came to visit with us; it was a great time. We learned that on that same weekend, Father's Day, my brother's children went to his home to cook a barbeque dinner for him, the first time in years. Our hearts were filled with joy.

October, I had a phone consultation with Michele and told her of the experience I had with the angels.

Michele then proceeded to tell me that the angels were all around me and would manifest for me on a photo. I should look for them, as they usually manifest themselves as odd colors and beams of light.

November, it was Thanksgiving time again and this time all the children were present and accounted for. The angels spoke and I will never doubt them again. Below you will see two photos each taken within seconds of each other in my basement that weekend.

The boy in the photo is one of my brother's children.

Arrival Notice

Within the past year our family lost two dear friends. In both situations I found myself praying for their easy passage into the light and for them to find comfort with the loving energy of God. In both cases within a few days' time while meditating I received communication that they were safe and with family. I did not communicate with them directly but a family representative would come through. The message was the same; We are safe and resting in the light, we hear your prayers. Love to all!

Prayer and Healing

Prayer is positive energy! All positive energies have a reaction on the physical. Your prayers have ability to heal yourself and others. Relax and think there have been times of healing.

Enjoy this!

There is so much about our brains and thoughts that is unknown. I am not a scientist or claim to know all. We have all heard of fabulous stories all over the world of miraculous healings that have taken place.

I have a theory on the power of prayer: You must believe strong enough in the possibility of the healing. You cannot just pray the words but must actually believe it. You visualize, breathe and taste with every cell in your body that this is possible. Your thoughts are energy and the light of God that is within us can heal. Visualize that beautiful white light surrounding the area of illness and purifying it. This energy creates a reaction and something happens! I would never say don't go to a doctor but I do believe that the power of prayer can assist modern medicine.

My husband's side of the family is from the beautiful Greek island of Kefalonia. They have a celebration in August for Saint Gerasimos; there are many stories of his famous miraculous skills of healing people with mental illness. Traditionally in Kefalonia, in the middle of August there is a religious ceremony. At this time, the saint's mummified remains are carried in a religious procession. There are many people with illness and/or troubles that sit in a line to have his remains passed over them for they believe strongly in his healing powers. My father-in-law and other locals have told me of witnessing healing miracles during this religious time.

What if the person who is ill or their loved one who brought them there, believed so much in the ability of this saint's power to heal, that their thoughts created energy for the positive healing reaction? I believe this is possible!

Ho'oponopono

I would like to bring to your attention the practice of Ho'oponopono. I know - Ho'opono WHAT? You probably never heard of it, nonetheless know how to pronounce it.

Ho'oponopono is an ancient Hawaiian practice of reconciliation and forgiveness. This is a practice to clear "stuck" energy and repetitive patterns not just within you but through the generations. This is accomplished with the use of a simple mantra;"**I love you. I am sorry. Please forgive me. Thank you!**"

I have incorporated Ho'oponopono into my prayer practice and have found it to be a wonderful enhancement. Although I do not teach this practice, for the purpose of explanation, I am providing you with my understanding because Ho'oponopono has helped me immensely along my journey.

In utilizing Ho'oponopono, the belief is that each individual is 100% responsible for what shows up in his or her life experience. Ho'oponopono is a process of clearing the stuck energy within. How? With the assistance from the divine and the use of the Ho'oponopono mantra.

When I clean my vibration I don't only clear my vibration but the vibration of life experience. In using this thought process, there is no finger pointing or placing blame on someone else for what is experienced. The practice of clearing stuck energy also clears repetitive and generational patterns.

Look at the words in the mantra. They are extremely powerful in their meaning and in their vibration:

I love you - unconditional love for myself and others. (Self love is a very important component.)

I am sorry – asking for forgiveness for whatever I have created, knowingly or unknowingly, in this lifetime or maybe even from the beginning of time. There is no need to understand or analyze it; Just acknowledgment that you are sorry.

Please forgive me - petition of forgiveness for those things mentioned above.

Thank you – have faith and believe that the divine (God, spirit, angels, guides, universe, whatever word you choose) has heard and will forgive and release this stuck energy.

This practice is simple, however we have a tendency to make it complicated by over thinking it.. Just try it and see how you achieve miraculous outcomes. (Additional Ho'oponopono prayer in Appendix B.)

<u>I Love You, I'm Sorry, Forgive Me, Thank You</u>

If you are interested in learning more about Ho'oponopono please go to this website http://www.self-i-dentity-through-hooponopono.com where you can seek out seminars affiliated with Ihaleakala Hew Len, PhD.

Chapter 5

Communication

Communication by definition is the exchange of information whether it is of thoughts or messages.

We are all energy, physical and spiritual beings that are here on this Earth plane for soul enrichment. The work of a medium is very valuable for we have the ability to connect the two dimensions. I would like to share with you my interpretation of the process.

This is done through a symbolic language. The components of this language are the enhancements of the senses already possessed:

1. sight
2. smell
3. touch
4. hearing
5. taste

During communication with a true medium the information received is correct and accurate; however, since this communication is received symbolically, the interpretation can be misinterpreted. This is why many times I will describe what I am experiencing and allow you the sitter to place the interpretation. When the message is right you will know it for IT FEELS LIKE A PUZZLE PIECE THAT FITS.

Many people think fortunetellers and mediums are one and the same; this is not the case. There is a big difference in the purpose and intention. A medium is not here to tell you your future but allow you to communicate and exchange energies with the next dimension. What is similar and may confuse the two are that there are validations given during communication. Since the next dimension is of a higher frequency and of a faster speed there is no sense of time and validations are given that apply to the past, present and future. My interpretations of these validations are as follows:

Validations of the past or present: Spirit is letting you know that they were with you at this time.

Validation of a future event: When the validation occurs, look back onto your notes for this is a validation of the communication that was given.

Always show your appreciation to spirit by thanking them. You can thank them directly through your own thoughts and prayers. Spirit is all around and can hear us.

To be able to express your feelings openly and exchange the thoughts from one being to another is communication. These thoughts assist in understanding and then growth and healing can begin.

The souls are happy to have the opportunity to communicate directly. They often try to communicate to their loved ones but unfortunately their efforts are dismissed as coincidences. To have the opportunity to connect with the intention of communication excites them as much as it does us.

You might have heard the expression he/she wears their heart on his/her sleeve. This refers to one viewing their feelings openly. For those in spirit this is the norm. The other side is all around us like the air in our existence. Your thoughts and prayers are heard. Open your mind and allow yourself to listen for their answers. The other side is one of thought, emotion and light. Their connection to us on the Earth plane is constant. We, however, don't acknowledge their subtle efforts to contact us. I would imagine that could be very frustrating. There is a very good book called *Hello from Heaven*, by Bill Guggenheim, Judy Guggenheim. I recommend it to all. This book is a collection and examples of many types of after-death communications. It is a wonderful book for those who have just suffered a loss, as well as, for those just interested in the subject, by sharing the unrelated experiences of how spirit tries to connect.

The work of a medium is thought of highly from those in spirit. It is the equivalent to that of a physician in our dimension, for growth and healing take place. To be able to share emotions freely opens the door for acceptance, appreciation, forgiveness, closure and the over all acknowledgment of existence beyond the life we know. This healing is on a soul level. Our soul is what we take with us from our existence to the next and the next. Therefore it is a step to eternal growth and healing of our souls' goal to be at one with the universal source of goodness.

Imagine when you go to a group session there are chairs of people waiting for an opportunity to hear from another in spirit. There are also many souls in the same room trying to get the medium's attention to be heard. It reminds me of getting on a bus in Greece or Italy. There is no line; everyone tries to get through the small doorway at the same time. For a soul to move through the dimensions to be heard, the soul must slow down their energy which takes a great deal of effort. I, in turn, elevate my energy and am assisted by my guides to receive and deliver the symbolic messages.

Spirit attempts to be recognized by shouting out names to get my attention. This could be a name of someone in spirit or someone on the Earth plane. Then to complicate matters it is usually a muffled name so I go with the sounds or initial. I don't like to get hung up on names but rather acknowledge the descriptions that are given. I in turn ask those who are sitting to raise their hands to show acceptance of the information given. Of course, if there is a common name given there will be more than one acknowledgment, so I ask spirit for further information and we can narrow down whom this communication is for. Spirit loves to multitask and in some occasions information is given that applies to more than one individual.

This communication is an exchange of energy and a collaboration effort is requested for those being read. In my opinion the medium should not ask a lot of questions and allow the information to come from spirit. This method will take a little longer but is more meaningful in the long run. The language is symbolic and I need to know if I am interpreting correctly. To determine this I ask the sitter for a **yes I understand or no I don't understand** without elaborating on details.

Above I explained the process of communication through mediumship. All forms of communication are of great importance from talking to each other in a daily manner or solving conflicts with understanding. The act of communication aids in understanding and allows love to enter the picture. Thoughts and energy are a common link between both worlds, Love being the highest level of energy and the energy life flow. During my progress I have been told by the higher energies that love is pure and never evil.

Please continue to heal each other and communicate in all aspects of life whether dealing with family, friends or acquaintances. Whether the communication tool is through thoughts, actions or words let us make a conscious effort for our communication to be of the highest level. If the subject is convoluted and you yourself don't understand where to start, try to break it down to the simplest level; it is all good and can be a beginning.

May all of our communications result in love, understanding and respect:

* Love is the easy part and in many cases unconditional.
* Understanding is the hard part, to understand differences between beliefs, traditions, culture, events, lifestyles etc.
* Respect means once we understand that there are differences we must respect one another.

Spread this thought process to another and then another; just plant the seed and let it grow on its own. It is not up to me or anyone else to change another; just plant the seed and open their minds to the idea. It is up to each individual to allow the seed to grow and prosper.

The ultimate goal would be Heaven and Earth on the same level of harmony and understanding. **Love, understanding and respect.**

No doubt we are a long way off, but what greater place to start than within.

Chapter 6

The Benefit of Seminars and Workshops

October 17, 2005

Education is what comes naturally. We express a thought or an idea that intrigues us then we proceed to pull the tools and means to find the answers. All questions have an answer; it is just waiting to be directed to you. Anticipate the knowing and then receive it. 1, 2, 3— knowledge, happiness, harmony and love intrigues us and builds our character one by one. The personality is the output of your soul. We grow and change to suit the environment that we live in. It is ok, never fear; we are all loved by God and the light which God rides through, the universe. Love and be loved.

<u>Workshops and Seminars</u>

I have been extremely fortunate to attend different events featuring well-known awakeners such as George Anderson, John Edward, Dr. Brian Weiss, James Van

Praagh and Abraham Hicks. I always felt the need to educate myself and what better way than to learn by experience? I have great respect for the work that they do and trusted my guides to direct me to their workshops.

George Anderson influenced me early on when I saw him on TV demonstrating his mediumship abilities. I related to his automatic writing techniques and then turned to his books. I loved reading about his experiences and the effect he had on others with his ability. After reading his work I could look at myself as useful instead of weird, realizing that there is a greater purpose for me. I had this ability for a reason but I did not yet know how to incorporate it into my life. My eyes were opened and I thirsted for more. I found myself being light-driven to other books and seminars. With each experience a new light was kindled inside.

Below I will share with you a few of my experiences and what I was able to appreciate and learn. It is my hope that through sharing these experiences you will kindle your own thirst for learning and appreciate your own experiences.

Participate in a Group Session with George Anderson

In 1998, I decided to go with a close friend Florence to see George Anderson. He had small group sessions with about twenty people in the room. I loved his books and was looking forward to this experience; the days could not come fast enough. The day finally came and it was a cold icy night in January. The three-hour car ride to Long Island gave me plenty of time to anticipate who might come through: my brother, grandparents— you know the usual relatives, but one of my thoughts was of a family friend named Kathy. Kathy worked with my husband and had been in my prayers for the past year. I wondered if George would mention her. Kathy came into money when her dad won the lottery and shared his good fortune. Even though she had this new-found security she could not hold onto it. Her heart was bigger than her wallet. Then to add insult to injury she died at a young age of cancer.

Once we arrived there was a noticeable excitement in the air. We could feel the energy; it was electrifying. The readings were random and not everyone had a chance to be read. Florence and I were both fortunate to receive a reading that evening. George discerned with great detail about my brother and grandmother. He stated that they were together, which was an answer to my mother's prayers. Then he asked if I take the name Kathy? She was family but in the form of a work family. She wanted to thank me for my prayers and asked that I tell the others I heard from her because she wanted to see their faces. Kathy knew that my husband and his co-workers were not very comfortable with this subject.

I had also received communication on my own from these loved ones but to get confirmation from a source I respected like George Anderson made that special experience even better.

What was learned by this experience besides the joy of communicating?

I am not trying to minimize the communications and the joy I felt when George delivered messages from my loved ones but I am writing about what I learned in addition to communication. I admired George's technique. Many mediums ask questions instead of trying to discern symbolic communication themselves. During the readings George did not ask a lot of questions; he asked the sitter to acknowledge if he or she understood the information that was given. He directed the sitters to only reply yes I understand or no I do not understand. This process might prolong the placement of symbolic discernment, but by having most of the information come from spirit the experience is more meaningful.

Second Visit to George Anderson

In 2002, I organized a group of twelve people to go see George. At this point I took great pleasure in sharing my experiences with others. The group consisted of my mother, sister-in-law Susan, Florence, friends and coworkers. For many it was their first time to see a medium and I was thrilled to share in their experience. Others in our group were related to each other, which was wonderful because there was greater chance for a communication to be experienced.

The night before our session, Mom, Susan and I were talking at the kitchen table, which is what our family does best—talk and eat. Mom was reminiscing about her childhood in nearby Philadelphia and eating chocolate cake. She was telling us a story about her neighbor and family friend Ceil. Ceil would have Mom come over for cake and taught her the art of eating chocolate cake. I never knew there was an art to eating cake but apparently if the cake is moist enough you could press the fork onto the crumbs allowing you to eat every last drop.

During George's session there were many visible healings taking place in the audience and the energy was very strong. George asked if anyone takes the name Ceil or Cecilia and nobody raised their hand. I suddenly looked at Mom and elbowed her to speak up. We were just speaking of her the night before and Mom was going to miss her opportunity. Mother very meekly raised her hand and Ceil brought through a wonderful reading that included many of our family members.

During the evening a soul by the name of Grace kept trying to come through but no one would acknowledge knowing her, therefore she could not move forward and deliver her message. This soul came back about three times during the three-hour session and was not recognized. Nonetheless, the evening was a success, many from our group received readings that night. My mother and Susan did receive messages which I also enjoyed, for their communications were from my loved ones as well. I enjoyed seeing the excitement in the room as people connected.

The next day I experienced communication in a very different way. I was in the kitchen with Susan and we were alone cleaning up the dishes. I started to notice flashes of white light around her head and I suddenly started to receive communication rather quickly through subtle thought. I was comfortable with Susan and therefore, I relaxed and told her everything as I received it.

He said, "My name is Rayford, like the town; my name and town are one and the same." He was a friend of her father's and came close to the family. He loved Susan like she was his own daughter and used to call her Suzie Q and also referenced bringing her fruit, especially apples. The reason for his communication was to tell Susan how much he and his wife Grace appreciated her kindness when they lived amongst us. He also mentioned that he and her father spend time together on the other side and both are well and happy.

When I finished Susan was amazed at what I told her. She sensed a familiarity of this information but was puzzled because she had not thought of these people in the longest time and as far as she knew Rayford was still alive. Susan immediately called her mother where she learned that Rayford had passed away two weeks prior. Susan's mom was able to verify all of the information. It turns out Rayford would tell everyone his name is Rayford just like the town. Rayford's wife Grace did not have any children and really appreciated their time spent with Susan and her family. Everything that was said was verified.

What was learned by this experience besides the joy of communicating?

What I experienced the next day with Susan in the kitchen was very significant because it was my first time I delivered communications using only thought. This communication was very clear and felt right. Plus we then realized that it must have been Grace coming through the night before at George's seminar but since she could not get acknowledged that evening sought acknowledgement the next day through me.

During communication, if you can acknowledge who is coming through whether it be a family member, friend, someone in the present or past, you should acknowledge them by raising your hand. If the communication is meant for you more information will clear up any possible doubt. If you don't acknowledge the energy there is a chance you may miss your opportunity and the conversation might not get initiated

It was from this point forward that I started communicating through thought rather than relying on automatic writing to bring thought.

Participate in a Seminar with Dr. Brian Weiss

I have been blessed with many experiences but one of the most fascinating to me was when I went to see Dr. Brian Weiss. Dr. Brian Weiss a renowned doctor and author who has done amazing work healing people through regression therapy and in doing so proves the existence of past lives. He also is instrumental in teaching meditation techniques. I had admired him through his books and was thrilled when I found out he was holding a seminar in New York, April 2005. As usual I uncontrollably informed others of the seminar. For some reason most of them could not make it but my two dear friends Keila and Florence were able to accompany me.

We booked the hotel and workshop. In the meantime another workshop opened up in Philadelphia, which was a more convenient location. Those that could not make it to New York were able to attend the March seminar. I decided all happens for a reason and planned to attend both seminars.

March, 2005—Philadelphia

This was amazing; there were a few hundred people in attendance but the experience was very powerful and all could experience at the same time. Everyone is at different level so as Dr. Weiss led us through the group regression, he explained that not all would report an experience right away.

Regression exercise

Think of a fond childhood memory; I thought of my grandparents' home. We were instructed to go back to our earliest happy childhood memory.

I was a baby in crib just brought home from the hospital. My two brothers were watching over me with total amazement and love of their new baby sister. I became overwhelmed with emotion. Please understand I am not the emotional type and usually don't cry easy. The emotion of love was so intense and overwhelming I could not stop my gushing tears from flowing. But they were not sad tears but ones of immense joy and love.

Suddenly I received a thought message from my brother Danny (who passed in 1995). He said, "I am always with you and continue loving you even now."

Dr. Weiss instructed us out of the regression and I regained my composure.

Then we were going to go back to our earliest memory beyond this life. We were instructed to look down and discover our surroundings.

I was in total darkness, dressed in rags; I was female. I could not see but I did sense my Dad and brother Danny were with me. We were in a leprosy pit. A man came toward us. I did not see his face but he was a Christ-like healer. This man came to heal my brother and I. Danny and I proceeded to leave the darkness of the pit into the bright light. As we stepped into the light I was stabbed in the abdomen and died by my brother's side. Suddenly I received thought messages from Danny again, He was with me then in that lifetime and I was with him in this lifetime and we will be together again.

Dr. Weiss then directed us to relate to what we saw in the regression to our current lifetime. How does this relate to my life now? The three of us—my father, brother and I—have a skin disorder, psoriasis. I have always been afraid of the dark. My brother passed at a young age and I enjoyed and loved his message to me.

Since this experience my skin has shown noticeable steady improvement.

Part 3

Taking Action

Chapter 7

Meditation Is Key

Meditation Communicating Within

Abundant is the ability to communicate; there is no charge in trying. People must open their minds to the possibilities and believe in the universal energy that surrounds all of us. Meditation is the key to success! If you open your mind and raise your energy you allow it to become a natural force from within. Remember not only do we have this energy inside us, but we have this abundant energy outside of our physical bodies as well.

This is the beginning of a new way of life for those who wish. Believe in your highest potential of loving energy, and all that is good. Enchanting is our life and it's full of natural wonders that are not yet understood. Take the step and try; like everything else that is of high value you must be patient and persist even if you do not achieve recognizable communication right away. What is important is the ability is there for those who wish to partake

How to Meditate:

Use the below structure as a guideline. You will eventually incorporate your own visualizations and timing to find what fits your individual needs.

* Find a quiet place where you will not be interrupted for about twenty minutes. Try to use the same place and time each day. (Be consistent and ritualistic.)
* Sit or lie down in a comfortable position.
* Quiet your mind and breathe relaxed deep breaths.

Relaxed Deep Breath:

a. Breathe in through your nose slow and steadily. Let the air fill your abdomen.
b. Hold the breath for a few counts.
c. Exhale slowly through your nose while deflating your abdomen. You can practice this method of breathing during the day until it becomes natural.
* Visualize a white light of protection surrounding you, keeping you safe and secure. You are totally surrounded by a loving energy.
* Focus on your breathing and bring a thought that gives you the emotion of love. When I first started, I thought of the loving emotion I felt from hugging my children.
* Play soft music without words. This will help to quiet the background thoughts that enter into your mind.
* With each breath imagine you are walking up a beautiful staircase (at least ten breaths).

* Once you have made it up the staircase continue with this relaxation breathing for a while (about ten minutes)
* When you are ready, come back down the staircase the same way you went up. With each breath imagine you are walking down the same beautiful staircase.

Cleansing Technique:

Once you get comfortable with the above process you can incorporate a cleansing visualization. This can assist you with the removal of negative debris.

Visualize as you breathe:

Breathe in the pure white light. Allow the light to enter from the top of your head and slowly with each breath visualize the light flowing through your body. Take your time and envision the light in your bloodstream reaching all of your organs and bones. With each breath you take allow the light to find and absorb the negativity like a sponge.

As you exhale, visualize the rubble and negativity moving far away to an imaginary place of restoration.

As you are coming to a close, imagine your body full of nothing but white light, totally clean. Ask to be guided on your path of the highest good, allowing only those who have your best interests at heart to approach you or influence you.

By meditating on a regular basis you can appreciate the uplifting effect it has on your life. For those of you who tried and then stopped due to difficulty in the beginning, you are not alone. Please try again and again. Be patient with yourself. Just like anything else, in the beginning it can be awkward.

A common excuse: "I can't quiet my mind, let alone breathe deep at the same time."

If you find it difficult to do this on your own, I suggest getting a guided meditation. You are welcome to use complimentary guided meditations available from my site www.2communicate.net or I recommend Dr. Brian Weiss, a renowned doctor and author, he has many wonderful guided meditations and regression audios. His work is wonderful and you will find his books among those that I highly recommend. Don't give up, take it one step at a time, one breath at a time, and with each breath you come a little closer to that harmony we call balance. Fifteen minutes a day is not too much to ask. Wake up fifteen minutes earlier in the morning. Everyone has their own pace so don't be frustrated with yourself. Some people may try every day for a month until they can successfully master this relaxation but the rewards will be great. This process can assist you on your road to physical and mental well-being.

Another common excuse: "I have an overwhelming and hectic lifestyle. I am too busy and stressed between working, school, social pressure and money to name a few."

This is a common situation and tends to pull your energy in many directions. I find with our lives being so hectic there is a tendency to lose track of the simple important things, such as unconditional love, communication, acceptance of others and positive reinforcement. Through meditation I have taken emotional and troubling situations and have been able to place them into a balanced clarity. Again, fifteen minutes a day is manageable for the busiest person and can make the world of difference. After mastering the technique of relaxation, utilize it to supply your soul with harmony and balance.

Anger

Like all emotions, anger creates a reaction. It is ok to be angry. However, try to understand why you are feeling angry. Sometimes you yourself don't know why you are feeling this way. Through meditation you can isolate and pinpoint your emotional direction. Once you have understood your feeling to the simplest form then deal with it through communication and understanding. Communicate with the one individual or group you have the issue with. Deal with it or accept its insignificance and get over it. **You must let the anger go. Release the negativity and you will feel better and more balanced.**

Countless problems have snowballed off a simple event that was not dealt with and therefore turned into a complicated mess. Find the root of the problem and isolate it. While entering your meditation ask for direction in finding a solution to this problem. The answer will come within time whether it is during your meditation or in your dreams. It is usually simple and one of few words. The subtle message tends to place clarity and balance onto the situation.

For example:

My husband, who I have known for more than half my life, loves me very much, but unknowingly through his actions, has been hurting my feelings repeatedly for more than twenty years. What I did not realize was his machismo ways would repeatedly put me at the bottom of the importance scale. His friends and work seem to take precedence over me and the kids. Although I know my husband loves us very much, in his heart he has difficulty expressing his feelings verbally. The bottom line is I have been ignored for more than twenty years and he has a tendency to be self-centered.

The same issue would resurface over and over again. I would react with angry words, never really dealt with these feelings and ultimately ended up suppressing my feelings. I always tried not to make a scene in public. Once we were in the privacy of our home the issues would be talked about but never really resolved. I allowed these feelings to fester inside and build. Eventually, I was not able to pinpoint exactly what it was that bothered me so much. I thought I was being tolerant and understanding, but what I did not realize was by bottling up this anger I made it worse. I unknowingly was holding this negative energy inside and creating a barrier. Every time I talked about him, jesting, sarcastic remarks would come out of my mouth. I found myself yelling and snapping for stupid things and I did not like the way I was behaving. I realized I had an anger issue, but was not sure how to deal with it.

I had recently (few months prior) begun the daily practice of meditation and decided to meditate on my healing of this relationship and added this situation to my cleansing during meditation. I wanted to cleanse the negativity and replace it with light of our highest good. One evening before I went to bed I prayed for assistance and guidance with this relationship.

That night I dreamt my stomach cramped and hurt. I went to the bathroom and started to throw up. There was no vomit. Instead I started to throw up a very large dead black rat! In my dream I understood that the rat was symbolic of my anger. The festering anger was gone. Through my dream I forgave the person and flushed the negativity down the toilet. When I woke from my dream even though I had been asleep my stomach felt sore. Emotionally I felt wonderful; I was uplifted, and relieved.

The negativity left and my daily meditation was improving I was able to achieve a higher energy level. A few weeks later, even though my meditation and frame of mind was improving, I was still not communicating with him the best I could. I decided to meditate on the subject for further clarity. What I received was the word *resentment*. What I did not realize was by holding that anger inside for as long as I did, resentment built up. I then asked, "How do I get rid of this resentment?" The answer I received was clear, *through love*. These two very simple words meant a lot to me and put everything into perspective. First of all I was too close to the situation to have a clear view and understand that it was me that was holding resentment inside. This thought of resentment never crossed my mind until my meditation. I thought once I dealt with the anger and forgave him that would be that. I decided to use the advice given through meditation and practice what I preach, love. Each time I started to say something sarcastic and or negative I would stop myself and focus on his positive qualities. Within a few weeks our conversations opened up in a more positive way. We were listening to each other instead of snapping angrily without finishing the conversation. Our relationship has improved immensely and on the road to healthier happier outcome.

My husband and I come from different cultures so acceptance and compromise has been a must for us from day one. He was born in Greece and came to this country when he was in his late teens. I was born and raised in the United States. He was brought up Greek Orthodox and I have been brought up Jewish creating a need for additional acceptance and understanding of our cultural differences. We have managed to raise three lovely children while sharing each other's faith, holidays, cultures and values. The bottom line to these obstacles is to look at our similarities instead of differences and build from there. Although we are from two different strong cultures, there is a common link of love that connects us.

Life is to be experienced and enjoyed

We are here on the Earth plane to express ourselves and share in the expression of others. Whether you are the one taking action or on the receiving end of another's actions, we are all connected to each other. This is why I implore you to make your actions, thoughts and words of a positive nature. Take your negative thoughts and turn them around to create a positive outcome. Granted, life is not always roses. However, if we take our thoughts and make only that which is good to be the end result, little by little your actions will achieve this result. Meditation can be a key to this intentional transition of positive thinking.

Recipe for a Great Day
(meditation 11-10-03)

Ingredients needed to have a great day:

- *Think with your head.*
- *Feel with your heart.*
- *Act with your hands.*

Think with the light of God in mind. Feel with God's love in your heart. Act human with God's understanding.

Chapter 8

Energy

"Love is to the soul like a fingerprint is to the body, an identifier. The more you love the better" (Through meditation 10-12-05).

This meditation is comparing the two dimensions:

1. Our dimension of the slower vibration, which is of a physical nature. We are all souls and identify one from the other in a material physical way by using our fingerprints.
2. In the world of spirit everything is emotion and thought. The highest level of emotion is love. Each soul is identified by their ability to love.

Our lives are intertwined not at the hip but within the air we breathe and the essence of our existence. Once we are born we start to breathe and there is life as we know it. Once we pass we stop breathing and our essences move towards the light. The light is our common link between the two worlds. The air is within the light and we are all beings of light just different levels of light-driven energies. To be light driven, *you are assisted by the energy force that loves us all collectively and individually. Whether or not you take this assistance or dismiss it is up to your free will. To recognize the light within you is one of the ways I hope this book will assist you. To be light driven is the ultimate expression of faith, to trust your inner self of that which is of the highest good.*

The two worlds, spirit world and ours vibrate alongside one another. This dimension (Earth plane) vibrates slower and is more physical, whereas the world of spirit is of a faster vibration and one of emotion and thought. Keep in mind our thoughts are energy. Thought creates a reaction; the reaction is emotion and each emotion vibrates on a different energy level. The highest possible level of pure energy is love.

The two dimensions coexist and have purpose far beyond our comprehension; we are a part of them and they are a part of us. When the soul realizes that there is a need to grow spiritually, the soul returns to this dimension for a crash course. This dimension is our school ground to experience emotions in a physical level.

We all have instincts; wild animals have instincts that assist them to survive environmental pressures, and sense danger. These animals are in touch with their inner selves. Humans however have that great gift of reason, choice and free will. Through these choices we experience our journey on the Earth plane and this journey is for our soul growth. We have chosen to experience many circumstances to help us with a predetermined understanding.

It was communicated to me that before being born we choose our soul lessons: what we desire to learn, our parents, entrance date and an exit date. There are predestining events or fate, for our life experiences. These events we must partake in for our soul growth and are life lessons that we have chosen from the other side. Our choices, free will, determine if we get to these predestined areas the easy way or the hard way. We are all souls; God's light and love is in each living being. It is up to us to develop and nurture our souls.

There are many religions in this world with many good ways of belief. I am not a theologian but would like to share with you a concept that I find to be truth. This truth encompasses all religions that believe in a higher power. This higher power loves unconditionally and vibrates at the highest possible level of good. Each being has a portion of this energy-light inside of us, our soul. Our soul is on a journey to achieve the highest possible level it can, which eventually joins the oneness of the pure loving light.

Energy is so complex yet very simple; look at our world as a whole the big picture; it is very overwhelming full of many types of energies, cultures and ideas. These energies vibrating on many levels full of different thoughts.

Energy, thoughts; how does this affect me?

We project energy through our thoughts, speech and actions. Energies that vibrate on similar levels will attract one another; this is referred to as the law of attraction. You probably have heard of the saying "Birds of a feather flock together". This expression supports the law of attraction by saying energies with similar vibrations and interests will associate with one another.

Did you ever walk into a room where people have been fighting and feel the tension? Did you ever hear the saying "The tension was so thick you could cut it with a knife"? This is energy that is affecting others. Our individual energy connects to our family and friends, which connect to our communities, our communities connect to our society, our society connects to our country and our country connects to the world, our dimension connects to the next dimension.

The other side or Spirit World communicates through a symbolic language. The souls are all around us and hear our thoughts and prayers. We are all related to each other in the vibration of the light.

If each individual took a moment to meditate and reflect on how their energy vibrates and the effect this vibration has on their home, work, etc., improvements could be made to attract only those of your highest good intent into your life. By assisting yourself and your vibration, you create a domino effect that affects others in the universe and raises the energy for the big picture and that of a greater good. No effort is too small!

Appendix A

This is what works for me, please use as a guide and find what works for you.

Protection Prayer:

The white light of truth surrounds us.
No harm will come to us
For we are all children of God.

Hear O Israel, the Lord our God, the Lord is One.

Our father who art in heaven hallowed be thy name. Thy kingdom come thy will be done on Earth as it is in heaven. Give us this day our daily bread and forgive us our trespasses, as we forgive those who trespass against us. Lead us not into temptation but deliver us from evil. For thine is the Kingdom the power and the glory forever.

Only those that come from God in love and peace may in any way approach us and or influence us.

Appendix B

This is a prayer I have been using and found very helpful along with the consistent use of the Ho'oponopono mantra; **"I love you. I am sorry. Please forgive me. Thank you!"**

MORRNAH'S PRAYER (Hawaiian Shaman)
Divine creator, father, mother, son as one...
If I, my family, relatives and ancestors have offended you, your family, relatives and ancestors in thoughts, words, deeds and actions from the beginning of our creation to the present, we ask your forgiveness...Let this cleanse, purify, release, cut all the negative memories, blocks, energies and vibrations, and transmute these unwanted energies into pure light....And it is done.

If you are interested in learning more about Ho'oponopono please go to this website www.self-i-dentity-through-hooponopono.com where you can seek out seminars affiliated with Ihaleakala Hew Len, PhD.